The Lord's Supper: Communion Counsel and Prayers

Edited by C. S. Foster

Copyright © 2006 Verbum Veritas
All rights reserved. No part of this publication may be reproduced, stored in a retrieval system, or transmitted in any form or by any means, electronic, mechanical, photocopying, recording, or otherwise, without the prior written permission of the publisher.

ISBN: 1-933899-01-8

Published by:
Holy Fire Publishing
531 Constitution Blvd. Martinsburg, WV 25401
www.ChristianPublish.com

Printed in the United States of America and the United Kingdom

Verbum Veritas
A Publication Ministry of Immanuel Lutheran Church
Murray, KY
www.verbumveritas.faithweb.com

Table of Contents

Prefatory Comments..7

I. Communion Counsel to the Newly Confirmed...........9
II. What the Lord's Supper Is..................................13
III. A Practical Examination before Communing.............17
IV. True Preparation for Communion........................23
V. The Salutary Use of the Lord's Supper...................27
VI. Christ's Purpose in Instituting the Lord's Supper......31
VII. The Benefit of Holy Communion..........................35
VIII. Why Do You Wish to Commune?.........................39
IX. Some Hindrances in the Way of a Worthy Partaking of Holy Communion..43
X. Do You Believe that You Are a Sinner?..................49
XI. Lord, I Believe; Help Thou Mine Unbelief...............53
XII. Follow Holiness...59
XIII. O Give Thanks Unto The Lord, For He Is Good!..........63
XIV. A Communion Meditation and Prayer....................67
XV. Why We Should Be Frequent Guests at the Lord's Table..73
XVI. Communion Counsel to the Sick...........................77
XVII. Additional Communion Prayers............................81

PREFATORY REMARKS

The counsel and prayers contained within the pages of this book can serve all Christians of any age. It is true that my initial audience is those whom I have confirmed or will confirm in the future, however, any Christian wishing to understand the Lord's Supper, the power of Holy Communion for their lives, and the centrality of the Eucharist within the context of worship will benefit from the wisdom of this book.

As a pastor, when I embark upon the very important task of catechizing our young, I have in mind four chief goals. First, I wish to provide a general, but thorough, introduction to the core of Biblical truth as understood by Lutheran Christians and instill within my confirmation students a true Lutheran identity. Second, I wish to foster and encourage parental involvement in the spiritual development of their children. Third, I wish to develop a personal and pastoral relationship with the catechumen (often, the time of confirmation is the first real exposure of a young person to the pastor outside of the Sunday morning service). Fourth, my goal is for the concluding confirmand to understand the sacrament of our Lord's Supper and to understand the concept of worthy reception and the centrality of this sacrament in our lives as redeemed children of God.

Through the public domain and the generosity of Immanuel Lutheran Church of Murray, KY, I am now able to offer my students (and the Church at large) the wise counsel and prayers of Francis James Lankenau (1868 – 1939) as contained in his 1935 work *Communion Counsel and Prayers* (CPH, St.

Louis). Dr. Lankenau has expressed the beauty, the power, and the mystery of our Lord's Supper far better than I could have hoped to pen myself. Hence, to the newly (and not so newly) confirmed, enjoy this classical work and may it help you in continuing a life-long relationship with Jesus and His meal. Amen.

The Rev. Dr. C.S. Foster
Immanuel Lutheran Church
Murray, KY
Easter 2006

I. COMMUNION COUNSEL TO THE NEWLY CONFIRMED

You are contemplating taking your first Communion. It is a most solemn step that you are about to take, the most solemn in your young life. You are to enter into most close and intimate relationship with your God and Savior. Such being the case, you should beseech God to grant you grace to receive His rich blessings in full measure. To this end may you, like young Samuel, meekly open your ears and hearts and say: "'Speak, Lord; for Thy servant heareth': Grant me the knowledge of Thy gracious truths and spiritualize the same by the blessed workings of the Holy Spirit that I may see Thy wondrous works and experience Thy boundless love to me and all sinners in Christ Jesus."

You have been faithfully instructed in the fundamental teachings of our Christian religion as revealed by God in the Holy Scriptures and so simply and beautifully summarized by Dr. Martin Luther in his Small Catechism. Thus you have learned to know how hateful sin is in your Maker's eyes, and the boundless grace of your merciful God in Christ has been pictured to you again and again. You have also received instruction in the important work of the Holy Spirit through the Word and the Sacraments, and you have experienced His regenerating and renewing power in your hearts. Especially has your pastor been insistent upon preparing you for your first Communion by telling you that the partaking of the holy Sacrament merely as an external act can be of no benefit to you. Be sure to spend some time in earnest meditation on these teachings and admonitions and thus seek to penetrate ever deeper into the depths of God's mercy and come to an ever livelier realization of the Savior's condescension in wishing to unite Himself more closely with you, a poor unworthy sinner. Then it will be most helpful to you by way of preparing you for your first Communion to review your whole past life as far as you can do so. Let your thoughts rest upon God's kindness and tender care, upon the many proofs of His love and the rich bestowal of uncounted blessings, and do not forget the many instances of His gracious protection and guidance when you were in dangerous and perplexing situations. Think of how often He has given you good things beyond your deserts and honestly acknowledge the many times His fatherly hand has preserved you from gross sinning and abject disgrace. Into how many a pit would you have fallen had He not sent His angels to guard your footsteps! How often would not vanity have led you astray had He not lovingly preserved you! In countless numbers of instances your evil desires would have brought you into situations that you must shudder to think of had not God's tender hand guided you aright. And then consider the heartaches your words and acts have caused your parents and teachers in numberless cases. Yes, by all means turn not your thoughts away from these sins of your childhood.

And if you follow this well-meant advice, your heart will be filled with shame and sorrow. Your disobedience and ingratitude over against God and your parents and teachers will humble you. But may you also be led to sincere repentance by the gracious working of the Holy Spirit, so that you will humbly confess your wrong to God and others whom you have offended! However, do not permit the contemplation of your many sins to end in despair, but rather seek refuge in the wounds of Jesus, who has redeemed you from all your sins by His holy, precious blood and His innocent suffering and death. Do as David did - ask our merciful God not to remember the sins of your youth, but to remember you for His mercy's sake.

And then, as you make ready to approach the Lord's Table, do not forget that you just have come from God's altar, where under most solemn circumstances you renewed your baptismal vow. You there promised loyalty and service throughout your life to God Father, Son, and Holy Ghost and renounced with equal earnestness allegiance to the devil, the world, and your flesh. This vow you made in the presence of many witnesses, before the assembled congregation, but particularly in the presence of the omniscient God. Do not forget that because of all the instruction, admonitions, and warnings given you, your God and Lord has a right to expect you to keep this vow, as He likewise has a right to see you grow in holiness and good works.

O my dear young friend, do by all means seriously consider these matters to which I have called your attention. Do not forget how your faithful pastor has on every possible occasion called your attention to these things because he was sincerely concerned about your spiritual welfare and had the hearty desire that you might derive the blessings of your first Communion in full measure and receive all the bounties of grace your Savior has in store for you in His blessed Sacrament.

PRAYER
O blessed Jesus, I know that I am a poor, lost sinner, but I also know that Thou hast redeemed me and in Holy Baptism didst bestow upon me the blessings of Thy redemption, accepted

me as Thine own, and made me the heir of life everlasting. Thou hast hitherto graciously kept me in body and soul, though I must admit that I have not appreciated Thy goodness as I should have done. And now Thou art about to add another unspeakably great blessing to all the other innumerable tokens of Thy love. Unworthy as I am, it is Thy intention to unite Thyself most intimately and mysteriously with me by imparting to me Thine own true body and blood under the visible elements of bread and wine in Holy Communion.

O Lord Jesus, I feel my unworthiness and realize my inability to grasp as I should Thy love and condescension. I pray Thee therefore, open the eyes of my faith that I may more clearly see the wonders of Thy grace and give me a larger understanding that I may penetrate more deeply into the unfathomable depths of Thy love.

And after having partaken of Thy precious body and blood, let me be Thine more fully in mind and body; let me cling more firmly to the precious assurance of Thy grace and enlarge my heart more perfectly in love toward Thee and my fellow-men. Grant me an increase of joy in Thy possession and a greater measure of courage to confess Thee before men by the testimony of my lips and the deeds of my hands. Yes, blessed Jesus, grant that my whole life may be a recognition that Thou art my Lord and help that my greatest joy may consist in serving Thee. Lord Jesus, here am I, let me be Thine forever, Thine alone. Amen.

II. WHAT THE LORD'S SUPPER IS

Our Catechism tells us: The Lord's Supper "is the true body and blood of our Lord Jesus Christ under the bread and wine, for us Christians to eat and to drink, instituted by Christ Himself." Thus in very simple language we are told what Christ gives us in His Holy Supper. These words of our Catechism are based upon Christ's own words as found in the gospels of Matthew, Mark, and Luke and in the First Epistle of Paul to the Corinthians. (Matt. 26:26-28; Mark 14:22-24; Luke 22:19,20; 1 Cor. 11:21-25.)

When Christ instituted this holy Sacrament, He took bread and wine and told His disciples to eat and drink these visible elements; but He also explicitly declared that with the bread and wine they were receiving His true body and blood; for He says, to use His own words: "This is My body, which is given for you; this is My blood, which is shed for you for the remission of sins." There is no truth more plainly expressed in Scripture than that Christ gives us His real body and blood with the bread and wine to eat and to drink. So plainly is this truth expressed that nobody can possibly err if he simply clings to Jesus' words. Besides the fact that these words are so simple and plain, they are repeated again and again to make it the more clear that Jesus wants them to be accepted in their simple and ordinary sense. But not even satisfied with this repetition, the Holy Spirit inspired the Apostle Paul to tell us, 1 Cor. 10:16: "The cup of blessing which we bless, is it not the *communion* of the blood of Christ? The bread which we break, is it not the *communion* of the body of Christ?" This can only mean that the very body which was given for us on the cross and the very blood that was shed for our redemption are united with the bread and wine as we receive these earthly elements in the Holy Supper.

Such being the case, it is clear, on the one hand, that we do not receive merely bread and wine in the Lord's Supper and that these earthly elements do not merely signify, or remind us of, Christ's body and blood; for if that were the case, there could be no *communion* of bread and the body of Christ or of wine and the blood of Christ in the Sacrament. On the other hand, it is equally clear that bread and wine are not changed into Christ's body and blood so that they lose their original nature and properties; for in that case it would also be impossible to speak of a *communion,* that is, a uniting of the bread with Christ's body or of the wine with Christ's blood in this Supper.

In some mysterious manner, altogether beyond our understanding, a union of the bread and wine with the body and blood of Christ takes place in the holy Sacrament, so that in, with, and under the bread and wine we receive Christ's true body and blood. Every communicant therefore can say in truth, "I have eaten Christ's real body and drunk His real blood."

Christ says: "This is My body, which is given for you; this is My blood, which is shed for you"; and we should by no means lose sight of these additional words, since they so very clearly express the blessed truth that in the Sacrament we receive the body that was given, and the blood that was shed, for our redemption, and they can thus only make us the firmer in our faith that we receive Christ's true body and blood in Holy Communion.

Of course, this is all beyond our power to understand; for how can our limited minds comprehend this incomprehensible mystery? But why should this trouble us since it is our kind and loving Savior, our true and ever faithful Jesus, the all-wise and almighty Lord, that assures us of the real presence of His body and blood under the bread and wine in the Sacrament? Why worry about understanding this impenetrable mystery so long as we know that it is just as the kind Lord Jesus tells us?

PRAYER

Dearest Jesus, Thy truthful lips assure me that in the blessed Sacrament Thou givest me Thy body and Thy blood under the bread and wine. I am fully satisfied with Thy assurance and do not doubt this real presence though my reason cannot comprehend it. Yes, Lord Jesus, I fully believe that Thou givest me Thy true body and blood in the Sacrament, the same body that was given for me on the cross and the same blood that was shed for my sins and transgressions, though all my reason and experience tell me that it cannot be so; for Thy word is more certain to me than my understanding and more valuable to me than all my limited experience. I pray Thee, keep me in this faith by Thy Holy Spirit for Thy mercy's sake. Amen.

III. A PRACTICAL EXAMINATION BEFORE COMMUNING

We all admit that we are sinners, and we daily see how we show this in our thoughts, words, and deeds. But often our sins seek to hide themselves from our eyes, or they wish not to be recognized as what they really are. Therefore the advice of Luther is a good one; he tells us that we should examine ourselves according to the Ten Commandments to learn about our sinfulness. This we should often do, but particularly should we do so by way of preparing ourselves for a salutary partaking of Holy Communion. And this we should do, not in a perfunctory and mechanical manner, but prayerfully and conscientiously.

PRAYER BEFORE EXAMINATION

Lord God, heavenly Father, enlighten my heart by Thy Holy Spirit, through the light of Thy Word, so that I may see my transgressions and sorrowfully admit them. Grant me also grace to make all possible amends where I have done wrong and to lead a more consistent Christian life to Thy glory. Hear me for Jesus' sake. Amen.

THE SELF-EXAMINATION

Do I truly believe in God Father, Son, and Holy Ghost? Do I recognize Him as the *only* God, to whom *all* divine honor belongs? Do I fear God so that I shun sin, even such sins as men cannot see? Do I fear God more than I do the opinion and ridicule of men? Do I love God more than any earthly person or thing? Do I also love Him when He visits me with chastisements? Do I trust Him above all things? Do I rest in Him and His promises in time of trouble, or am I needlessly anxious? Is it actually so that I do not trust more in men or my own resources than I do in God?

Are God's Word and His holy Sacraments dear to me, and do I use them as I should? Do I carelessly or profanely use the name of God? Have I cursed by God's name? Have I been guilty of needless swearing by God's name? Have I sworn falsely or blasphemously?

Have I used magic or the services of spiritualistic mediums and of fortune-tellers? Have I made light of holy things? Have I been indifferent in matters of doctrine, and have I acted toward those who have departed from the truth of God's Word as though it were a matter of no importance to do so? Have I been sincere in my confession of the truth and in my daily life? Do I often approach the Throne of Grace in prayer? Do I neglect my morning, evening, and table prayers? Do I cultivate a grateful spirit, and have I thanked and praised God as I should for all His benefits?

Have I been a diligent and devout worshiper in God's house, or am I easily persuaded to absent myself from divine service? Am I a frequent and devout communicant at the Lord's Table? Have I sought to retain and practice what I have heard in the sermon? Do I regularly contribute to the Lord's kingdom and as the Lord has prospered me? Am I an active member of my Church and congregation? Do I seek to bring in the unchurched? Do I try to set right the erring and comfort the distressed? Do I use God's Word regularly in my own home? Am I a regular private Bible-reader?

Have I been respectful and obedient to those whom God has placed over me in church, school, state, and home? Have I always borne in mind that they are God's representatives and as such worthy of honor and reverence? Have I been properly grateful to my parents and my other superiors for their many services? Do I show my love for my parents by deeds of kindness to them and by caring for them in their old age? Have I shown disrespect to my parents by entering upon a betrothal or marriage without their consent or even against their will? Do I remember my superiors in my prayers as I should? Do I take the proper care of my dependents bodily and spiritually? Do I properly instruct them in the ways of God's commandments? Do I set them a good example?

Am I envious, resentful, and easily aroused to anger? Have I sinned by means of violent gestures or words and thereby offended or harmed others? Have I done harm to others by injustice, carelessness, neglect, or some uncharitable act? Have I held a grudge against others and been unwilling to forgive or seek reconciliation? Have I undermined my own health by immoderate eating and drinking, by immoral living, penuriousness, or overwork? Am I kind, cheerful, humble, and meek in my intercourse with others? Do I pray for those who have wronged me? Do I gladly help the poor and needy?

Do I love and honor my spouse? Have I been guilty of gross sins against the Sixth Commandment? Do I nourish unchaste thoughts by reading indecent books and magazines or by attending salacious moving pictures and shows? Have I been guilty of making unseemly gestures or of speaking unclean words? Have I done things that must shun the light of day?

Have I sought to overcome unchaste thoughts and desires by the use of God's Word, prayer, temperance, and work? Have I always shunned the indecent exposure of my person, pride, indolence, immodest dress, filthy singing, and dancing?

Have I always been fair and just in my dealings with others? Have I been guilty of theft or sharp dealing? Have I taken advantage of others in buying and selling? Do I try my utmost to pay my debts? Have I been careless in contracting debts? Do I envy others their prosperity? Am I saving without being penurious? Have I been guilty of gambling and speculating?

Have I defended others as I should? Have I prayed for them? Have I returned evil for good? Have I been kind to others, even at the expense of some sacrifice on my part? Do I like to listen to gossip, and am I even a gossiper myself? Am I always careful to speak the truth? Have I been sincere and upright under all circumstances? Am I careful to verify evil reports that come to me about others before I pass judgment? Do I rather speak good than evil of my neighbor? When a witness in court or at other times when making sworn and other statements, have I always realized that God hears what I say and is an Avenger of falsehood?

Do I always seek to overcome the covetous thoughts that arise in me? Do I have an inordinate desire for honors, wealth, praise, and recognition? Do I sincerely seek the welfare of others?

Have I wasted my time and opportunities to do good? Do I seek to use my talents in the service of God and my fellow-men, or am I only intent on applying them for my own advancement and gain?

Do I always bear in mind that I am God's because He created, redeemed, and sanctified me and that for this reason all I am and all that I have belong to Him and should be used in His service and according to His will and direction?

Have I always looked to God for guidance? Do I ask Him to enlighten my mind and direct my will, and do I then follow such light and direction?

Am I fully convinced that I am a sinner? Do I really believe that I am a lost and condemned sinner? Do I sincerely believe that only Jesus can save me? Do I actually believe that He has saved me?

PRAYER

O Lord God, I see my utter sinfulness and helplessness. I was conceived and born in sin and have been guilty of transgressing Thy holy commandments day by day all my life. I know that because of my sins I deserve Thy wrath and punishment and am in no way worthy of Thy love and kindness. I have no excuses to offer for my transgressions and will not insult Thy holiness and justice by seeking to belittle them or by asking Thee to pardon them because of my sorrow and tears. But I come to Thee in Jesus' name and ask Thee to be merciful to me because He shed His precious blood and died for me upon the cross. Yes, O Lord, for Jesus' sake be merciful to me a poor sinner; and as Thou givest me strength, I promise to better my life and to pass my days in increasing measure to Thy glory. To this end I beseech Thee also to bless my contemplated Communion that it may become more and more apparent that Christ liveth in me and I in Him, to the praise of Thine eternal love, Jesus' unbounded grace, and Thy Holy Spirit's blessed activity. Amen.

IV. TRUE PREPARATION FOR COMMUNION

The Lord's Supper is no ordinary meal, such as we daily partake of; it is even far above the richest banquet a king might prepare for some honored guest; for in it we are given Christ's true body and blood under the visible elements of bread and wine. Since this is the case, it must be plain to every one that we should properly prepare ourselves lest we receive bane instead of blessing and death instead of life.

When the Lord descended in the cloud and passed before Moses, Moses bowed his head and worshiped, Ex. 34:6, 8. Here in the Lord's Supper, however, we not merely see the Lamb of God, but we receive Him, His body and blood. When Uzzah (2 Sam. 6:7) put his hand on the Ark of the Covenant, which only priests and Levites were allowed to touch, he immediately died; how much more should we be careful lest we eat and drink damnation to ourselves by unworthy partaking of the bread and wine in the Lord's Supper, since here is the real body, of which the Ark was only the shadow!

Hence Paul tells every Christian who contemplates going to the Lord's Table: "Let a man examine himself, and so let him eat of that bread and drink of that cup." Such an honest examination will bring out our weaknesses and unworthiness, our sinfulness and damnableness, and show us that we deserve God's wrath and punishment in time and eternity.

But as we thus come to a realization of our own unworthiness and vileness, let us not lose sight of the fact that God nevertheless wishes to make us the objects of His boundless grace in Christ, the Beloved. Of this we are assured by the blessed bread and cup, which are the communion of the body and blood of the very Lamb of God that taketh away the sins of the world and which very body and blood are given us in the Sacrament. Surely He that makes us partakers of His body and blood cannot wish us harm. This blessed truth let us accept in childlike faith and say: "God would be merciful to me, a sinner, and to this end He gives me the very body and blood which gained my forgiveness. In the holy Sacrament He gives me all the blessings of Christ's redemption, forgiveness of sins, life, and salvation."

PRAYER

O Lord God, heavenly Father, I know I am most sinful and unworthy, and Thy all-seeing eye can behold even more than is revealed to me. I am not worthy to be called Thy child and would not dare to do so if Thou in Thine unlimited grace didst not assure me of my acceptance as Thy child in spite of all my disobedience. So, also, I see how unworthy I am to come to the table which Thou hast prepared for us and where Thou wilt give us the body and blood of Thy Son under the earthly elements of bread and wine. How can I, who am sinful from the crown of my head to the sole of my feet and whose every part of body and soul is defiled, presume to become the dwelling-place of my Savior? It is only the assurance of Thy Word that I am a welcome guest that gives me courage to come with all my sins and unworthiness. Yes, it is because I trust in Thy grace and in Jesus' atonement for my sins that I come just as I am, poor and wretched, seeking the riches of Thy forgiveness and the comfort of Thy love. Grant that I may receive the blessings I humbly and believingly seek, for the sake of Jesus Christ, my Lord and Savior. Amen.

V. THE SALUTARY USE OF THE LORD'S SUPPER

In His Holy Supper the Lord Jesus gives us most precious treasures. He there grants us gifts without which we shall be lost in all eternity. When He instituted His Supper, He whose lips cannot lie declared: "This is My body, which is given for you; this is the new testament in My blood, which is shed for you for the remission of sins." Not only do we orally receive Christ's body and blood, but as we receive these in, with, and under the consecrated bread and wine with our mouths, we also receive by faith what His words declare, namely, the forgiveness of sins. Were we merely to receive Christ's body and blood with our mouths, it would have been sufficient for Him to have said, "This is My body; this is My blood." But He says more. Not only does He tell us that He gives us His body and blood, the very body that was given and the very blood that was shed, but He adds that His body was given and His blood was shed *for us.* The Lord Jesus not only desires that we eat His body and drink His blood, but He desires us believingly to consider that His body was given for us and His blood was shed for us *for the remission of our sins;* yes, He seals and emphatically confirms this by giving us to eat and drink the very body and the very blood that merited this forgiveness for us. And we know, where there is forgiveness of sins, there is also life and salvation. These are the precious treasures which Christ gives us in the Holy Supper, and without these we should be forever lost. For we are sinners, who have transgressed God's Law, and by our disobedience we have deserved His wrath and displeasure, temporal death, and eternal damnation; but these treasures, imparted to us in the Sacrament by the word of promise, make us rich and eternally happy.

And all this is given us without money and without price; for no merit or worthiness on our part is expected or demanded. What the labor of our hands cannot do, what our gold and silver cannot buy, Christ gives us freely in the Sacrament: Forgiveness of sins, life, and salvation.

But as we should not seek to pay God for these treasures of grace, so also we should not doubtingly ask, "How can this be?" or carelessly think, "I do not need these gifts"; but by God's grace we should overcome all vain self-righteousness by pondering upon our own spiritual helplessness and subdue all rising doubts and dulling indifference by pondering upon God's great love as manifested in the Sacrament. Such thoughts will then fill our hearts with gratitude and cause our lips to overflow with praise to God for the priceless riches He bestows upon us in His Supper. This humble and believing contemplation of God's love will then lead us to regard the Sacrament as a true Eucharist, an act of thanksgiving, and cause us whole-heartedly to join in singing: "It is truly meet, right, and salutary that we should at all times and in all places give thanks unto Thee, O Lord, holy Father, almighty, everlasting God:" And after partaking of Holy Communion, we shall heartily pray: "We give thanks unto Thee, almighty God, that Thou hast refreshed us through this salutary gift:"

God grant that we may thus believingly and gratefully partake of the Lord's Supper at all times!

PRAYER

Almighty and eternal God, I am about to approach the table prepared for me by Thy dear Son, my Lord Jesus Christ. I come as one that is sick to find healing; as one unclean, to be cleansed; as one blind, to receive sight; as one poor, to be made rich. I pray Thee, grant that I may find healing, cleansing, sight, and riches; help that I may humbly and reverently, with due sorrow and devotion and childlike faith, approach the holy Sacrament and thus receive Christ's body and blood unto my salvation and ever be numbered among the members of His spiritual body in time and eternity. Also help that I may so use the Sacrament that the fruits of Christ's redemption may be shown in my daily life to the praise of His holy name. I ask this for Jesus' sake. Amen.

VI. CHRIST'S PURPOSE IN INSTITUTING THE LORD'S SUPPER

In Holy Communion Christ gives us His body and blood under the bread and wine for the forgiveness of out sins. As we use the external, visible elements according to His institution, we are made partakers of His grace and salvation. By thus uniting His invisible blessings with the visible elements, His purpose is to come to the assistance of our weak faith. The very blood of Christ which was shed to institute and confirm the new covenant of grace is given us in the Lord's Supper as a lasting memorial of His atoning death upon the cross. As often as we eat the bread and drink the cup in Holy Communion, we show forth the Lord's death; that is, we declare that He died for us and all sinners and that His death is in full effect until the end of days. The Lord's Supper is ever reminding us of Christ's vicarious and atoning death and telling us that our main care should be the publishing of this sacrifice for the sins of the world from day to day as opportunity is given us.

The Lord Jesus expresses the purpose of the Lord's Supper very plainly Himself in the words "Given and shed for you for the remission of sins." By these blessed words the Savior tells us that His body was given into death that we might live and that His blood was shed that we might be cleansed from our iniquities. He wants us Christians to eat His body and drink His blood that we may eternally live. Oh, the great love of the Savior, who thus seeks in every way to further and secure happiness and salvation!

Let us ponder deeply upon these gracious intentions and

purposes of our dear Savior as we make preparation to approach His table. Consider His tender solicitude for us by tying up His grace with the visible elements in the Sacrament that thus our doubts might vanish and our weak faith be strengthened. How ungrateful it would be on our part not to acknowledge this kind purpose of the Savior! Then, too, remember that it is the blood of the New Testament, or New Covenant, which Christ gives us in the Sacrament; for it is just this fact that should assure us of His grace as long as we trust in His holy, precious blood that was shed for us.

May we also remember that Christ wants us to show forth His death for us when we eat and drink His body and blood; and may we let this thought impel us frequently to approach the table of His grace, since the gratitude of our heart for Jesus' atoning death should cause us to glorify our Savior's redeeming love by word and deed. And then let us not forget that Christ instituted the Sacrament of His body and blood that it might be a pledge and seal of our intimate union with Him through faith in His merits; and may this thought also be a strong incentive to us for a frequent approach to His table, since all of us, as sure as we are Christ's and have felt the sweetness of being His, must have the heartfelt longing to become ever closer to Him who is the Source of all pure pleasure. In one of our hymns we sing:

> Jesus, priceless Treasure,
> Source of purest pleasure,
> Truest Friend to me!
> Long my heart bath panted,
> Till it well-nigh fainted,
> Thirsting after Thee.

> Thine I am, O spotless Lamb!
> I will suffer naught to hide Thee,
> Ask for naught beside Thee.

But how can these words be truthfully uttered by our lips if we do not make diligent use of the very means by which He would bring us to an ever greater certainty that He is our Jesus and we are His own? By Holy Communion, Jesus would take us into His arms, calm all our fears, and assure us of His protection against all the foes that seek to molest us. Surely we should be showing ourselves most unappreciative to our Savior and should be depriving ourselves of untold blessings if we did not use His Sacrament as He bids us do.

PRAYER

O Lord Jesus, how unspeakably Thou dost love me, and how earnestly dost Thou long for my happiness and salvation! Thou gavest Thyself into death, into shameful death, even into death upon the cross, to atone for my sins and to make me acceptable in the eyes of Thy Father. But Thou desiredst to do still more -- Thy boundless grace has prompted Thee to give me in Thy Holy Sacrament a further proof of Thine all-absorbing interest in my welfare in order to strengthen my weak faith and confirm the covenant of Thy grace. In this Sacrament Thou dost impress upon me that I should never forget Thy death for my salvation.

I cannot sufficiently thank Thee for Thy goodness, since it is impossible for me to measure its height or depth, its length or breadth; but I pray Thee, help me that I may at least in a small measure see and acknowledge Thy boundless love as I approach Thy table. Strengthen my weak faith and give greater ardor to my love for Thy mercy's sake. Amen.

VII. THE BENEFIT OF HOLY COMMUNION

Christ, the loving Savior and almighty God, has spread for us a rich and blessed repast in the Holy Supper. All the blessed fruits of His redemption He there sets before us for our spiritual delectation. Actuated by His boundless love, He not only assures us of our redemption in the Gospel, but in the Sacrament actually communicates to us the very body and blood given and shed for our salvation.

This unlimited grace should be ever in our thoughts as we approach His table, so that we may always remember that all His merits, the whole fruit of His redemption, are there offered, given, and sealed unto us. The simple acceptance of the Savior's words in which He tells us that He gives us His body and blood, the very body and blood given and shed for the forgiveness of our sins, gives us this blessed assurance. In the Sacrament we eat the very body that was nailed to the cross and that died for our transgressions, and we drink the very blood that was shed for the atonement of our sins. In giving us His true body and blood, Christ gives us all that He gained for us by His suffering and death. In other words, Jesus and His atonement, His perfect holiness and righteousness, His merits and full redemption, are fully and freely given us. Here is indeed grace above measure and love beyond comprehension. But it is really and truly just as we have said; for Christ's own words in unmistakable language assure us of the blessed fact.

A further special benefit derived from the Lord's Supper is that we are thereby assured of a most intimate communion with all believers on earth; for at the Lord's Table we are all partakers of the one bread and the one cup. And this thought must be most uplifting for us and cannot but strengthen our faith that by believingly partaking of Christ's body and blood we all become partakers of the salvation which He has merited for us. No matter how greatly space, race, language, or condition in life may separate us, in the Holy Supper there is an invisible, but indissoluble tie, a tie that binds all believers together in the one faith in the one Savior.

And as our partaking of Holy Communion strengthens our faith, so it also increases our love to God and our fellow-men. Just in proportion as our faith in Jesus' merits grows, so the new life of love and service will become stronger, and we shall grow richer in good works. Without Jesus we cannot truly love and serve God and our neighbor; but if we are united with Jesus, we cannot fail to grow day by day in the service of love.

And finally the partaking of the body and blood of our victorious and exalted Savior cannot fail to increase and foster our hope of life eternal. In receiving Christ's body and blood, we cannot but be confirmed in our trust that He will not fail to fulfill in us His promises: "I go to prepare a place for you," and: "Where I am, there shall also My servant be."

Oh, are not the benefits which the Savior gives us in His Holy Supper wonderfully great and precious? Is not the grace there offered rich beyond measure? But let us mark well that only the believing guest receives these blessings; while the body and blood are received also by the unbelieving communicant, only the hand of faith can appropriate the riches of His grace, forgiveness of sin, life, and salvation. May we therefore approach the Lord's Table with a serious, though not downcast, mind and with a humble, though cheerful, heart, fully aware of our own unworthiness, but no less certain of Jesus' merits. May our one desire be to receive the benefits and blessings Christ offers us in His Sacrament!

PRAYER

Dearest Jesus, in Thy Holy Supper Thou hast prepared a feast that is able to supply all the wants of my soul; here Thou wouldst give me food and drink to strengthen my weak faith, to impart new ardor to my love, and to enliven my hope of life everlasting. I know, Lord Jesus, that much of these intended blessings is lost to me because of my weakness; but I pray Thee not to hold my frailties against me. Rather grant me an increased measure of Thy Holy Spirit, so that by the enlarging of my faith I may be able more fully to partake of the riches Thou wouldst impart to me by partaking of Thy Holy Supper. Hear my prayer for Thy love's sake. Amen.

VIII. WHY DO YOU WISH TO COMMUNE?

Jesus says: "Blessed are ye that hunger now; for ye shall be filled," Luke 6:21. This is also true of those who go to the Lord's Supper with hungry souls. Those who hunger after righteousness shall experience that Christ is the Fount of all fullness. They shall taste and see that the Lord is gracious. Them He will feed with finest wheat, and He will fill them with marrow and fatness. With great delight will they learn that His fruit is sweet and most refreshing. Of His fullness He will give them grace for grace.

And yet, how many of us go about lean and poor and in rags; how weak and withered are our graces! But this is not because He has failed us; it is rather because we have failed Him. Our desire and our hunger for Him fail, and it is for this reason that we are not filled with the good things we so greatly need. Jesus Christ is the same yesterday, today, and forever. His supplies are as plentiful now as they were a thousand years ago, and He will continue to offer us a full and rich supply to the end of time. His table is ever ready, and it is richly furnished to satisfy every hungry soul.

But we are often so hesitant and lacking in spiritual appetite. We frequently act as if His food were not good enough for us. He calls, and we come not; He invites us, and we ignore His pleading. And when we do come, we are not hungry for His grace, and His food is not to our taste.

What is the cause of this lack of hunger on our part? Why this indifference to the rich banquet spread for us in the Lord's Supper? We do not appreciate God's grace because we are blind to the hideousness of our sins. We long not for the assurance of God's pardon because the damnableness of our transgressions is not present with us. We long not for the fullness of Christ's mercy because we do not feel empty. We seek not amnesty from the King of kings because we do not recognize that we are guilty of treason. We have no desire for the garments of Jesus' righteousness because we see not our shameful nakedness. We have no longing to be washed in the fountain of Jesus' blood because we are ignorant of our foulness.

Oh, that God would give us hunger, so that He could fill us! Blessed are they that hunger, for they shall be filled. God make us truly hungry lest we perish for want of Christ, as is the case with thousands. Yes, may Christ make us truly hungry, so that, in giving us His own body to eat and His blood to drink, He can fill and strengthen us! He longs to enlarge the desire of our souls. He would not have us be content with crumbs; no, He would feast us with His fullness. His hand is overflowing with riches; may our hand be held out to receive the treasures intended for us! While the dear Savior has already given us more than we had a right to ask, He wishes us to want more still. He yearns to have us say: "I long to come into ever fuller possession of the riches of Christ's grace, know Him and His will better, appropriate Him with all His merits more fully, and serve Him more loyally."

If we come thus hungry to His table, the all-gracious and bountiful Savior will surely say to us: "Ask what ye will, and it shall be done unto you. Open your mouths wide, and I will fill them."

PRAYER

Lord Jesus, make me truly hungry for Thy love, which I do not merit, but of which Thou wouldst make me more certain in Thy Holy Supper. Fill me ever with longing for the food and drink of life to which Thou hast so tenderly invited me; and as I partake of Thy body, which languished for me on the cross, and drink of Thy blood, which was shed for my sins, may I never forget Thy love, dear Savior! Jesus, Bread of heaven, nourish my weak faith with Thy strength. Savior, Thou Fount of every blessing, increase my love to Thee and my fellow-men. O Lord God, grant my humble prayer for my good and Thy glory! Amen.

IX. SOME HINDRANCES IN THE WAY OF A WORTHY PARTAKING OF HOLY COMMUNION

The heart of a communicant should be centered upon his Savior and upon those great blessings which He intends to bestow upon him in the Sacrament, for which reason all those things that might hinder him in this should be banished from his mind. Sorrows and worries concerning earthly things may so weigh down our hearts as wholly to deprive us of the intended benefits of our Communion. If we permit Satan to fill our hearts with doubts as to God's help and protection in earthly things, how can we rest securely in the thought that in the Holy Supper Jesus will make us partakers of all His merits? If we cannot trust God to care for our bodies, how can we have confidence in Him to provide for the wants of our souls? Surely we must have faith in the Lord for the little things before we shall be able to rely upon Him for heavenly and eternal blessings. It will therefore be necessary to permit the Savior's blessed assurances of His abiding help to expel from our hearts all distracting fears lest they deprive us of the sweet blessings intended for us in Holy Communion.

In close connection with our worries concerning temporal matters is our secular work and business. God, of course, does not want us to be slothful in business. On the contrary, He insists that we Christians be models of industry and application. But our work must not occupy our thoughts to the exclusion of spiritual and heavenly matters. After all, the sunshine that has its source in God's grace and Christ's redemption should glorify all we think and do, and as we approach His table, we should seek to center our thoughts and desires upon Him and do our utmost to turn them away from our daily work lest we lose that rest and peace for our souls which Christ has gained for us by His labors and which He wishes to communicate to us in the Sacrament.

In particular should we shun all thought and desire for sinful appetites and indulgences. Let us have our thoughts journey to Calvary, and there, at the foot of the cross, let us kneel in deep humility and contrition, resting our eyes upon the bleeding head, sad countenance, and tear-dimmed eyes of our blessed Savior. And as we do so, may this sight drive away every thought of carnal pleasure from our hearts and banish every sinful pastime from our minds! While there are many pleasures and pastimes that are harmless in themselves, they do become positively harmful if we permit them to dominate us; especially do they become harmful if they distract our thoughts and disturb our minds as we approach the Lord's Table and thus cause us to lose the great blessings God can pour only into the attentive and receptive heart. Do, then, by all means close the door of your heart to all that might divert your attention and devotion in the holy hour of your Communion.

Even more will we hinder, yes, prevent Christ from making us the recipients of His intended blessings if we approach His table with anger, enmity, and implacability towards our fellow-men in our hearts. It should not be necessary to have our attention called to the fact that a heart filled with hatred and kindred thoughts is closed to the benefits of Holy Communion; for in the very nature of things it must be apparent that a heart filled with enmity and hatred has in it no room for the love of Christ. On the contrary, it must be apparent to everybody that such a heart is ruled by the thoughts and desires of an unworthy communicant, who will eat and drink damnation unto himself. Christ cannot possibly welcome us to His table if enmity instead of love fills our hearts; for if we come to Holy Communion, which is the feast of His love, in a spirit of hatred and implacability, we make a mockery of Him whose love for us and whose longing for our forgiveness led Him to give His body and shed His blood on Calvary's cross. Besides, let us not forget that one of the main purposes of Christ in instituting this Sacrament was that by the communion of His body and blood we communicants might be more closely bound together by the mutual bond of love in Him whose love constrained Him to give Himself as a sacrifice for us. Yes, we who in the Holy Supper partake of the sacrifice of our Savior's love unto the strengthening of our faith and thereby become most intimately united with Him and with one another, how could we possibly harbor hatred and enmity in our hearts towards those with whom we have become one or towards any one whom Christ has redeemed by His blood? No, no; as we approach the altar, we must not forget that Jesus bade us love one another and forgive one another. The sad fate of the unforgiving servant in the parable who lost his master's forgiveness by his refusal to cancel the debt his fellow-servant owed him should ever be a warning to us, also our daily prayer: "Forgive us our trespasses, as we forgive those who trespass against us." Therefore let us pray God to help us overcome all anger and enmity towards our neighbor for the sake of Christ's love to us.

But we cannot close this meditation without considering those persons who are in a state of doubt concerning their worthiness. Not a few of these are quite probably really unworthy. They are negligent in the private and public use of God's Word; they are disobedient children or unfaithful parents; they are unkind, unchaste, indecent, dishonest, and they frequently sin with their tongues against their neighbors. And they are not really sorry for their wrong-doing, though they may be vexed because one or the other sin they have done has resulted in bringing them grief and trouble. For these persons there is but one thing to do, namely, to learn in the light of the Ten Commandments and of Christ's suffering and death on the cross how hateful and damnable sin is and by God's grace to become truly penitent before they approach the Lord's Table.

But there are also other persons in a state of doubt as to their worthiness. They are those timid souls who feel that they are not as sorry for their sins as they should be or who realize how weak their faith is. Such doubting souls, for one thing, should remember that their sins cannot possibly be greater than Jesus' redemption; on the other hand, they should hold fast the blessed truth that God's grace and their salvation are in no way dependent upon anything that they must do. God's Word is clear in telling us that, mighty as sin may be, God's grace is mightier and that, though our sins be as scarlet, they shall be as white as snow. These trembling hearts can do no better than cling to what St. John positively affirms: "If any man sin, we have an Advocate with the Father, Jesus Christ the Righteous," and they should never forget that it is just those who are groaning under the burden of their sins whom Jesus gives the assurance: "Come unto Me, all ye that labor and are heavy laden, and I will give you rest." Yes, it is these above all that Jesus would have come to His table and say: "Dear Lord, we are poor sinners and therefore come to Thy

Holy Supper trusting fully that for Thy sake we shall receive forgiveness for all our sins." They will be welcome guests, since it is especially for such timid, sorrowing hearts that He has instituted His Supper that there they may find comfort and refreshment.

PRAYER

Lord Jesus, as I approach Thy table, I find my mind not so free from earthly concerns as it should be, and these earthly matters greatly disturb my devotion and threaten to deprive me of Thy heavenly blessings as offered me in the Sacrament. To my great distress I also see that in my heart there is not that full desire to forgive those who have wronged me as it should be found in a Christian's heart. And I likewise find that my contrition is not so deep as it should be and my hatred of sin is far from perfect. But just because of my imperfections I come to Thee for grace, forgiveness, and strength. O blessed Savior, grant me grace to prize the treasures which Thou wouldst bestow upon me by Thy flesh and blood in the Sacrament as immeasurably more precious than all the satisfaction that the world can give me; tear out all bitterness and enmity from my heart and make me meek and loving and forgiving; overcome my doubts by the assurances of Thy Word and Sacrament; and fill my soul with a longing for the heavenly food and drink to which Thou hast so graciously invited me. Yes, Lord Jesus, make me truly hungry and thirsty for Thy grace and then grant me sweet refreshings at Thy table for Thy mercy's sake. Amen.

X. DO YOU BELIEVE THAT YOU ARE A SINNER?

This is the first question which our Catechism in the "Christian Questions" asks those who intend to go to the Sacrament. The answer it gives is: "Yes, I believe it; I am a sinner." Every communicant should have this firm conviction. And how is it possible that any man should want to deny this fact? Have we not all been guilty of baseness, ingratitude, insincerity, and dishonesty? Have we not daily despised our heavenly Father's power, wisdom, and goodness? And what indignities have we not heaped upon our Lord Jesus! His body was cruelly torn with nails and His precious blood was spilled by His murderers; but have we not occasioned Him more grief and sorrow by our many sins? They crucified Him but once; we, however, have crucified Him daily by our transgressions; they sinned because they knew not what they did, but we have sinned against Him whom we knew to be our Savior and our Lord. We have stubbornly resisted the gentle pleadings of the Holy Spirit, opposed His strivings, and destroyed His work. Truly, we are full of disease, sin, and pollution. So vile are we in the light of God's holy Law that we are not worthy to come near Him, much less to come and sit down at His table. Laden with sin, we are not fit to draw near this holy feast which divine grace has prepared. We have so often abused God's grace, our hearts were often so cold, when they should have glowed with holy rapture. Oh, that we could shed sufficient tears mourning for our sluggish hearts that are so little moved by the Savior's suffering! The Son of God weeps and bleeds for us, and we weep not as we should for our sins, which pierced His brow with thorns, His hands with nails, His side with a spear, and His heart with sorrows. Lord Jesus, give me a penitent heart since Thou givest assurance that Thou wast exalted for the very purpose of giving repentance to Israel.

Oh, that we might realize our unworthiness to sit at His table! Oh, the amazing love of God that He should kindly invite whom He could command and, in case of disobedience, punish instantly with eternal hell-fire; that He should take poor slaves, condemned to the prison of hell, and make them crowned kings of heaven; that He should not only save us from hell by giving His life on earth, but feed us with the very body and refresh us with the very blood by which He saved us! These are truly prodigies of love, which should constrain us to love our Savior and mourn for our sins while we live.

PRAYER

Lord Jesus, I humbly confess that I am a vile sinner and wholly unworthy of Thy mercy. But Thou didst graciously accept the publican's prayer, the tears of the woman who was a great sinner, the faith of the thief on the cross, and the repentance of Peter. By these examples of Thy mercy I am encouraged to draw near to Thee. Oh, send me not away empty lest I faint by the way. Satisfy my needy soul with the food of Thy heavenly banquet that I may receive spiritual strength and nourishment unto eternal life. Yes, O Lord, hear my cry and hide not Thy face from me; as Thou hadst respect to the people of Nineveh when they humbled themselves unto Thee, so turn also in mercy to me. Dost Thou not invite even those whose sins are as scarlet to come to Thee, and dost Thou not assure them that Thou wilt cast out none that come to Thee? And are not many thousands who have experienced the truth of Thy Word at this hour singing Thy praises and exalting Thy free grace?

Lord, make also me a monument of Thy grace; have pity on a repenting and returning sinner; take me to Thy table and make me Thine forever, so that I may become a loving sacrifice to Thee, who didst offer Thyself a dying sacrifice for my redemption. Hear me, Lord Jesus, for Thine own sake. Amen.

XI. LORD, I BELIEVE; HELP THOU MINE UNBELIEF
Mark 9:24

Faith in Christ is always clothed with humility. The higher the thoughts a man has of Christ, the lower the thoughts he will have of himself. And so, too, as a man learns to know his own nothingness, by the grace of God his eyes will be opened to see the holiness and excellencies of his Lord Jesus. The knowledge that our own righteousness and merit are worth nothing in the eyes of a just God is used by the Holy Spirit to direct us to the Lamb of God, which taketh away the sin of the world, and to assure us that forgiveness can be had only by our appropriating Christ's sufferings, death, and atonement. This all-important truth will then bring home to us the fact that only he is a welcome and worthy guest at the Lord's Table who has faith in these words: "Given and shed for you for the remission of sins." While we must indeed realize that it is truly too great an honor for such guilty and filthy creatures as we are to be entertained by a spotless Savior as His guests, yet our humility must not induce us to doubt our welcome, though we see nothing in ourselves to commend us to Him. While fully aware that we sinners are vile in the sight of a holy God and that all our righteous acts are as filthy rags, yet this conviction of our unworthiness must not tempt us to reject the dress of Jesus' righteousness in which He so graciously offers to clothe us as His guests at the heavenly banquet He has prepared for us. Of course, we are insufficient for anything that is good; but the Holy Spirit in the Sacrament desires to work in us both to will and to do of His good pleasure. Jesus is under no obligation to pity or help us; but since He, in His free mercy, offers us the very help we need, we should gratefully accept "the righteousness of God in Him" and permit Christ to array us in the glorious dress of His blood and righteousness. We should look to Christ as our Surety and be willing to live wholly upon borrowed and imputed righteousness and strength; trusting in His assurances, we should live upon Christ Crucified and ask from Him, hour by hour and day by day, strength and righteousness for duty and difficulty, for work and warfare.

And we should firmly believe that in Holy Communion the very body that was given and crucified and the very blood that was shed for our redemption are truly present and given us to eat and to drink under the consecrated bread and wine. Thrusting aside all doubts because of our own unworthiness and disregarding all other difficulties that reason may present, we should build our faith firmly upon the love, omnipotence, omnipresence, faithfulness, wisdom, and truth of Christ, who can and will give us His body and blood in the Sacrament as pledge of His forgiveness, as He has promised. To doubt the presence of the Savior's real body and blood in Holy Communion would be to offer Him an insult in view of His positive assertion.

Finally, our faith should also hold fast this blessed truth, that, as Christ's sacrifice of His body and blood for the sins of the world was accepted by the Father as full atonement for our sins, so the Father in the Holy Supper imputes to us the merits of Christ's body and blood just as certainly as He gives us this body and blood in the Sacrament. This is the specific purpose of the Lord's Supper, to assure us that all the blessings of Christ's redemption, forgiveness of sins, life, and salvation, are ours just as certainly as we receive the body and blood of the Lamb of God that was slain for us. This faith is based on the Word of God, which stands firmer than the everlasting hills; for heaven and earth may pass away, but God's Word never will pass away. And even when Satan tries to induce us to imagine, in a spirit of false humility and lowliness, that our vileness and pollution are greater than God's mercy can possibly be, let us not succumb to such temptation, but rather overcome it by firmly clinging to, and building on, the promises of God's Word. Though God's mercy may indeed be a marvel in our eyes, since He so highly honors us instead of dealing with us as we deserve, yet let us ever hold fast to the fact that He *is* offering us free pardon through Christ's blood and is calling us to His table. While we are not worthy to stand among God's lowest creatures, He bids us sit down with His children and gives us, who deserve not to eat the food of men, to partake of the body and blood of His Son; and since God does this in His boundless goodness, let us not in false humility refuse the riches of divine grace. With joyful hearts let us accept the blessed invitation extended to us and trustingly receive Christ's body and blood as a seal of our pardon. Yes, let us come and eat with gratitude towards Him who was bruised, ground, and scorched that He might become a Bread to nourish our starving souls; let us come confidently to the repast which divine grace has so bountifully provided to give us boldness and cheerfulness of faith. May we keep our eyes centered upon Christ's promises as given us in His Supper and never lose sight of the fact that they are the words of Him who never failed to speak the truth! Let us not permit our own weaknesses to deprive us of the sweet comforts He wishes to give us in the Sacrament, but be encouraged to wait and hope, since He has promised not to forget the needy nor to let the expectation of the poor perish. In due time the measure of our joy will be increased, and our weak faith will become stronger as we faithfully use the Sacrament according to the Savior's will.

PRAYER

"Lord, I believe; help Thou mine unbelief." So I feel constrained to cry as I am about to approach Thy table. As the Searcher of hearts Thou knowest that my faith is very weak and that doubts often disturb my thoughts. But, dear Lord Jesus, I cling to Thy Word and rest in Thy omnipotence and truth. I ever have before me Thy assurance that in the Sacrament Thy body and blood are given me and, further, that they are given me for the remission of my sins. I am overcome by the thought of my unworthiness and readily confess that I have deserved Thy wrath and punishment, temporal death, and eternal damnation. But since Thou hast said that Thou givest me Thy body which was given for me and Thy blood which was shed for me, I come to Thy table in full confidence that Thou wilt hold communion with me, as Thou hast promised. It is difficult for me, who am so impure, to grasp the magnitude of Thy grace in thus coming to me and providing for my guilty soul full pardon. Thy favors to me an unworthy creature are incredibly great; but I doubt them not, though I am unable to grasp them with my senses, for to me Thy Word is sure. As I think of what I deserve at Thy hands and of the assurances of Thy love, I find it hard to realize that the cup of blessing, filled with hope and pardon and eternal life, is actually intended for me; but I pray Thee, increase my weak and wavering faith by Thy Holy Spirit and let it grow to an ever stronger confidence and a fuller capacity to enjoy Thy blessings. Help me in an increasing measure to appreciate the glory of Thy grace in the Sacrament and drink with ever greater satisfaction the cup of salvation which Thou hast purchased with Thy blood and sweetened with Thy blessing. Hear me, Lord Jesus, hear me, for Thine own sake. Amen.

XII. FOLLOW HOLINESS
Heb. 12:14

The believing Christian will follow holiness; that is, he will seek to better his life. A necessary fruit of a God-pleasing Communion will be a walk more consistent with God's will and commands. The communicant who approaches the Lord's Table without having the good and earnest purpose to better his sinful life is manifestly an unworthy guest. The very nature and purpose of the Lord's Supper tells us this. For is not the Lord's Supper a memorial of the Savior's death for our sins? How can we, then, worthily partake of the body that was given into death for our sins and of the blood that was shed for our forgiveness, if we continue to love sin? Surely, if we believe that Christ died for our sins on the cross, we shall realize that we ought to crucify our flesh and cease from serving sin. It would certainly be most inconsistent under these circumstances for us not seriously to determine to serve our Lord Jesus by seeking and striving to become more faithful in the performance of our duties; more fervent in our love to God, more consistent in our fear of Him, more upright in our trust in Him, more sincere in our prayer, more zealous in the reading and hearing of God's Word, more God-pleasing in our thoughts and desires, and more loving and kind in thought, word, and deed toward our neighbor, more humble, more meek, more chaste, more unselfish, more truthful, and more edifying in our whole conversation.

The price of our redemption was exceedingly great, for we were not redeemed with perishable silver and gold, but with the holy, precious blood of God's own Son and His holy, innocent suffering and death. And this sacrificial body and blood, the very price of our redemption, Christ gives every communicant in the Sacrament under the blessed elements of bread and wine to eat and to drink as the pledge and seal that he has been delivered from sin, death, and the devil and that forgiveness of sin, life, and salvation is his. How the partaking of this purchase price must strengthen his faith, comfort him in distress of body and soul, and urgently admonish him to dedicate his life to Him who redeemed, purchased, and won him from all the enemies of his soul that he might be His own and live under Him in His kingdom and serve Him as his Lord and King!

The unbeliever, because he is an unbeliever, is not ready to recognize Jesus as his Lord, but puts his body into the service of vanity and selfishness, compels it to satisfy his carnal desires, and uses his powers for dishonoring his Maker, harming his neighbor, and destroying himself. The believer, on the contrary, adorned as he is with the blood and righteousness of Christ, desires to put all he is and all he has, his eyes, ears, tongue, hands, and feet, into the service of his Savior. His constant wish is to praise his Redeemer by his daily conversation. He knows that righteousness and unrighteousness cannot agree, that light and darkness can have no communion, and that Christ and Belial have no concord, and therefore he will most zealously seek to have his heart cleansed from all those things which are displeasing to his Lord and are inconsistent with one who through faith has been united with the Lord Jesus.

Of course, the believer daily sees to his great chagrin and distress that the deed falls far short of the wish and that he does not serve his Savior so fully in holiness and righteousness as he would. While he knows that Jesus died for him and rose again, that he should henceforth not live unto himself, but unto Christ, his Redeemer, he finds his flesh ever opposing his good desires and trying its utmost to hinder his making progress in holiness. But this should not lead the believer to become despondent and give up the strife with the devil and his flesh in despair. Rather should this continuous opposition of his enemies be an incentive to him more diligently than ever to use the God-appointed means for the strengthening of his faith, namely, the Word and the Sacrament. And God, who has bidden him use these means, will make true His promises; He will not only keep him in the true faith, but will strengthen his faith and grant him more and more strength from day to day to follow holiness. If he continues the strife in the strength which God gives him through His Word and Sacrament, He will grant him new courage and vigor to walk in the ways of His commands, and he may rest assured that the Holy Spirit, who has begun the good work in him, will not forsake him, but continuously grant him His help and comfort. God never has forsaken, nor will He ever forsake, those who trust in Him and show their trust by using the means of grace which He has ordained to make and keep them His own.

PRAYER

Dearest Jesus, I have often promised Thee when I came to Thine altar that I would mend my sinful ways; but, alas, how lamentably have I failed to keep my promises! Again and again have I succumbed to the promptings of the flesh from within and the temptations of the world from without, and how often has Satan with his deep guile succeeded in bringing me to fall! O dear Savior, I am so weak and frail, and all my attempts at betterment can only fail in the future if Thy grace does not come to my rescue. Without Thee I can do nothing. Because I know this, I once more take courage to come to Thy Supper; and as I come, I beseech Thee: "Create in me a clean heart, O God, and renew a right spirit within me. Cast me not away from Thy presence and take not Thy Holy Spirit from me. Restore unto me the joy of Thy salvation and uphold me with Thy free Spirit." I bring to Thee, Lord Jesus, the sacrifice of a broken spirit and a contrite heart and pray Thee not to despise it. Believe me when I tell Thee that I earnestly intend and purpose to follow holiness, and I humbly beseech Thee, strengthen my will and grant me grace to cast away the works of darkness and to walk in Thy light. Help me to crucify the Old Adam within me by daily contrition and repentance and grant the new man new strength to live in righteousness before Thee. Bless my Communion and thereby help me to carry out my resolution to turn my eyes from beholding evil and to prevent my lips from speaking guile; also help me to close my ears to what is offensive to Thee and make my heart the dwelling-place of holy thoughts and righteous desires. If I should stumble, keep me from falling; and when I grow indifferent to the dangers that threaten my soul, remind me, as Thou didst Thy disciples, to watch and pray. Dear Lord Jesus, I beseech Thee to hear my humble prayer. Amen.

XIII. O GIVE THANKS UNTO THE LORD, FOR HE IS GOOD!
Ps. 118:1

The Christian who has partaken of the Lord's Supper has particular reasons to extol the goodness and mercy of God; for he has there received as a pledge and seal of His redemption the very body and blood which secured him his salvation. His ears have heard the blessed assurance that Christ's true body and blood have been given him as a token of the forgiveness of all his sins. Thus has been brought to his heart a firmer conviction of his redemption from sin and misery, and his hope of life eternal has been strengthened. For all these blessings he should loudly sing the praises of his God and Lord.

Oh, believing communicants, give the Lord thanks and express your gratitude both by your words and by your actions. Highly esteem your Redeemer and His blood and righteousness, through which such inestimably great blessings have been purchased for you. Avoid everything that dishonors Him and flee from sin as you would from a plague. Commend your Redeemer to those who know Him not by bearing witness of Him and of His truth and grace in the midst of a Christ-despising generation. Pray and work for the enlarging of Christ's kingdom and rejoice at every victory your King Jesus wins over the powers of darkness.

Show your gratitude by singing psalms and hymns and spiritual songs in praise of Christ's redeeming love, of His person, His offices, and His sufferings. Sing praises to the great God, who left His throne on high and came down to dwell in the flesh to die for us, and magnify the glory of Him who rose from the dead for our justification and ascended to glory in heaven to take possession of His inheritance and there to make intercession for us. This singing of praises to your Savior King is most acceptable to God and profitable to you. Yes, "sing praises unto God, sing praises; sing praises unto our King, sing praises." As God makes the singing of praises the eternal employment of the saints in heaven, so He would have us frequently employ it on earth, particularly after we have partaken of the soul-nourishing and faith-quickening Supper of our Lord. Again we say, let us give thanks unto God for His unspeakable gift now and forever!

PRAYER

Blessed Jesus, in deepest humility and heartfelt gratitude I give thanks to Thee that Thou hast granted me poor sinner the privilege of sitting at Thy table, that there Thou hast nourished me with Thy body and refreshed me with Thy blood, and that Thou hast made me an acceptable guest by clothing me, through Thy Holy Spirit, with the wedding-garment of faith in Thy merits. O Lord, I confess that I am wholly unworthy of all the blessings Thou hast bestowed upon me in Thy holy Sacrament; but the more deeply do I appreciate Thy goodness, and the more earnestly am I concerned about giving Thee due thanks for Thy great condescension and grace. Gracious Savior, accept the offerings of my Lips and despise not the gratitude of my inmost heart. I am truly grateful to Thee for Thine atoning death and for Thy merits, which Thou hast so graciously imputed to me by faith as I partook of Thy body and blood in the Sacrament. For all Thy mercies I praise Thy holy name.

Blessed art Thou for having filled the hungry with good things and for having quenched the thirst of my soul. I dedicate my whole life to Thee and Thy service, and that day I shall count lost on which I forget Thy love. Help me to grow in faith and love and hope. Deign to make me Thy temple and grant me strength to consecrate all my powers to Thy service. Hear me for Thy name's sake. Amen.

XIV. A COMMUNION MEDITATION AND PRAYER

Dear Lord Jesus, as I approach Thy table, I shall endeavor to think of all my needs and wants to lay them before Thee; and I humbly pray that out of Thy fullness Thou wilt grant grace upon grace.

What I most of all desire is the full forgiveness of all my sins. When I think of my transgressions, I am ashamed to lift up my face to Thee; for against Thee have I sinned most grievously in thought, word, and deed. My transgressions are more than can be numbered. Which of Thy commandments have I not broken? In what hour of my life have I not offended Thee? When I think of all my sins, I can but exclaim with the psalmist: "Who can understand his errors? Cleanse Thou me from secret faults." I am heartily sorry for all the sins I have committed against Thee and have nothing to plead in extenuation for my transgressions. There would be no peace and no hope for me if Thy blood did not cleanse me from all sins. All my trust I place in Thy grace and mercy as my Redeemer. I know I have often abused Thy mercy in the past and am not worthy to apply again for the cleansing by Thy blood, which I have so often treated with contempt and trodden under foot. And yet, what can I do, and whither can I go but to Thee? Therefore:

> Just as I am and waiting not
> To rid my soul of one dark blot,
> To Thee, whose blood can cleanse each spot,
> O Lamb of God, I come, I come.

The Scriptures assure me that Thy blood is able to wash away stains of the deepest dye, and so I, "though tossed about with many a conflict many a doubt, fightings and fears within, without," come to Thee and beseech Thee to let me experience the blessed power of Thy blood upon my soul. Lord, be it unto me according to Thy Word. I pray Thee to look upon my wretchedness and misery and have mercy upon me for Thy merits' sake. I have broken all the commandments of God; but Thou hast kept them all in my stead. I have offended God's justice, despised His goodness, abused His patience, and deserved His wrath; but Thou wast bruised for mine iniquities and wounded for my transgressions; the chastisement of my peace was upon Thee, and therefore I trust that the merits of Thy righteousness will be upon me. I flee to this city of refuge and lay hold upon the horns of this altar and will not let Thee go until Thou bless me. And further I pray, though I am but dust and ashes: Seal Thy pardon unto me by the communion of Thy body and blood in the Sacrament, of which I am now to partake, that I may be able to exhibit it to Satan and my own accusing conscience and thus defy their attempts to deject and terrify me.

And then, Lord Jesus, grant me Thy grace in every hour of need.

> Just as I am, poor, wretched, blind;
> Sight, riches, healing of the mind,
> Yea, all I need, in Thee to find,
> O Lamb of God, I come, I come.

All my springs are in Thee; without Thy grace I must languish and die; without Thee I can do nothing. I wish to live by faith in Thee; I would have you take possession of my heart and abide there. Lord, increase my faith; help mine unbelief. May the holy Sacrament of which I am about to partake be an earnest and pledge that Thou wilt grant my prayer. Grant that by faith I may put my finger into the print of the nails that pierced Thy hands and feet and lay my hand into Thy side, so that thus I may be fully persuaded that Thou hast suffered and died for me. In mercy grant me grace to say with Thomas, "My Lord and my God!" and with the happy spouse, "My Beloved is mine and I am His."

Lord Jesus, shed abroad Thy warm love into my cold and frozen heart; inflame it with fervent affection and desire for Thee that I, too, may be a disciple whom Thou lovest and be numbered among those who love Thee in spirit and in truth.

Dear Lord, grant me also a greater measure of spiritual knowledge. Thou knowest that my mind is darkened by sin, and I am naturally estranged from Thee through the ignorance that fills my heart. For want of keen spiritual sight I am guilty of many mistakes. O give me understanding that I may know Thy will; shine into my heart and give me an ever fuller knowledge of Thy glorious Self.

Give me also humility of spirit that I may not exalt myself above others. Keep my heart from swelling with foolish pride and vanity at every fancied or real elevation or preferment. And as I would have Thee graciously preserve me against haughtiness on the one hand, so also preserve me against insolence and fretfulness at every disappointment. Lord Jesus, give me a greater portion of Thy humility and meekness and help me to imitate Thy lowliness of spirit.

O Lord Jesus, do not grow impatient with me because of my importune asking. I must confess that I have not that deep sense and full conviction of my great sinfulness that I should have and wish to have, and therefore I ask Thee to give me more godly sorrow for sin. Remove my stony heart and give me a heart of flesh that I may despise myself for all my transgressions and iniquities. Give me greater purity of heart and a more spiritual mind that I may draw nearer to Thee and be more fit to be in Thy presence. Grant me a greater hunger and a deeper thirst for righteousness. I know that Thou art more than willing to feed the hungry and give water to the thirsty, but I find that Thou must give me the hunger and thirst as well as the food and drink. Lord, give me this appetite and desire that I so greatly need just at this time as I am drawing near to Thy table. As the hart panteth after the water-brooks, so my soul panteth after Thee, O Lord.

But my prayer is not yet ended. As I meditate upon my wants, I find that I need more gratitude for all the mercies I have received at Thy hands. Let me not be indifferent to Thy food and drink, but grant me grace to show my appreciation for all Thy loving-kindnesses by satisfying my soul with the marrow and fatness which Thy grace sets before me at this banquet and help that my mouth may praise Thee with joyful lips.

Grant me more patience and contentment in every condition of life; give me more wisdom and prudence; bless me with greater courage and resolution; arouse me to greater activity and zeal. Cure my blindness, remove my impenitence, dispel my unbelief and hypocrisy, banish my deadness and formality, and replace my inconstancy and backslidings by firmness and loyalty.

O Lord, what is it that I do not need? But this is my comfort --
I cannot want for anything that Thou canst not give me. Yea,
Thou knowest of what things I am in need before I ask Thee
and art able to do exceeding abundantly above all that I can
ask or think. Therefore with full confidence I say:

> Just as I am, Thou wilt receive,
> Wilt welcome pardon, cleanse, relieve;
> Because Thy promise I believe,
> O Lamb of God, I come, I come.
>
> Just as I am, Thy love unknown
> Has broken every barrier down;
> Now to be Thine, yea, Thine alone,
> O Lamb of God, I come, I come.

Amen.

XV. WHY WE SHOULD BE FREQUENT GUESTS AT THE LORD'S TABLE

The Apostle Paul complains that so many of the Corinthian Christians did not make proper preparation before going to the Lord's Supper. We today must make the same complaint and to it add another, namely, that so many of our members commune so very seldom. Not a few of our people go to the Lord's Table only once a year and some not even that often. This is greatly to be deplored.

But what should admonish and incite a Christian to receive the Sacrament frequently? Our Catechism answers this question thus: "In respect to God both the command and the promise of Christ the Lord should admonish him and in respect to himself the trouble that lies heavy on him, on account of which such command, encouragement, and promise are given."

Christ tells us in the words of institution of the Lord's Supper: "This do in remembrance of Me," and again: "This do, as oft as ye drink it, in remembrance of me." Twice the Lord tells us: "This do." This repeated command should make it clear to us that going to the Holy Supper is not a matter of indifference, not a thing that we Christians may do or not do, as it may please us; for earnest and insistent is the divine command "This do." It makes it our sacred duty frequently to commune at the Lord's Table, even as His command makes it our bounden duty gladly to learn and hear His Word. The negligent and infrequent use of the holy Sacrament in spite of this explicit command would be most reprehensible disobedience on our part and bring us great spiritual harm.

But another reason why we should frequently commune is to be found in Christ's gracious promise. The believing communicant is promised indescribably glorious riches and blessings in the Lord's Supper. For hear what Christ says: "Take, eat; this is My body, which is given for you. Take, drink ye all of it; this cup is the new testament in My blood, which is shed for you for the remission of sins." These words tell us that the Lord's Supper is a true love-feast wherein Christ most wonderfully reveals His infinite love; a banquet of grace where Christ wishes to embrace us with His boundless grace; a heavenly table where He will give them that are His to eat of the eternal manna and to drink of the river of His pure pleasure. Every laboring and heavy-laden sinner is told by these precious words that to assure him of the forgiveness of his sins, the Savior gives him the very body that died for him on the cross and the very blood that was shed on Calvary for him and all sinners. To make us sure that really all our sins are forgiven, completely forgiven, and that life and salvation are ours, the Savior instituted this holy Sacrament before His death as a memorial of His atoning sacrifice and as a pledge and token of our redemption. Because of Christ's promise, as found in these words of institution, every believing communicant may exult: "As surely as Christ orally gives me in the Sacrament the very sacrifice He offered for my sins and the ransom He paid for my redemption, so certain am I that God is my gracious heavenly Father and heaven my eternal inheritance." In view of the glorious heavenly gifts and treasures offered and presented to all who come to His table trusting in His promise should it be possible for any among us not frequently to come to the Sacrament to receive the offered treasures and riches of divine grace?

But there is yet a third reason why we should be frequent guests at the Lord's Table, and that is the trouble that lies heavily upon us. This trouble of ours is sin; for we Christians are still sinners and daily sin much. So much and so seriously do we sin that we can have no idea of the number and the greatness of our transgressions of God's Law. But our sins, even our sinful thoughts, are deserving of God's wrath and displeasure. And since such is the case, we stand in daily and continuous need of forgiveness; for which reason we must often be assured: "Be of good cheer, your sins are forgiven." Of course, we have received forgiveness in Holy Baptism, and we are offered it in every Gospel sermon and in every absolution; but must we not admit that we often have doubts as to our forgiveness? Is it not often a difficult matter for us to say with firm confidence, "I believe that Christ has redeemed me and that all my sins are forgiven"? Now, it is just because the blessed Savior foresaw these doubts that He in His boundless love to us instituted His Holy Supper therein to assure us of the forgiveness of all our sins and thus to strengthen our weak faith. And such being the case -- in view of our weak faith and God's boundless love and His concern for our eternal welfare, which prompted Him to add this Sacrament to Baptism and the Gospel, so that thereby rest might be given to our troubled hearts and confidence be brought to our trembling souls -- should we not hasten to this blessed table of God's grace to receive the priceless boon that is intended for us? Should we not have a longing desire frequently to partake of this Sacrament and there to rid ourselves of the heavy burden of sin?

May the Lord Jesus by His Holy Spirit lead us to be frequent and worthy guests at His table, to be filled with a sincere longing for pardon and grace; and may He further grant us grace to depart from His altar with the blessed assurance that our sins are forgiven!

PRAYER

Dearest and most merciful Savior, Thou art the eternal Son of the Father and yet didst not disdain to come into our wretchedness and misery to save us; yes, Thou dost even call us sinners Thy brethren, and now in Thy exaltation Thou bearest our nature as an eternal proof of Thy love. And Thy love prompts Thee not only to live among us, but even to dwell in our sinful hearts and to make our souls Thy temple and home.

O Lord, what are we that Thou shouldst thus honor us? Help that we may not despise Thy grace and cast from us Thy love. Grant that, as Thou dost graciously invite us to Thy table of grace, we may not despise Thy will nor reject Thy mercy. Give us hearts that will obediently heed Thy command and open our eyes to see the greatness of our sins and the riches of Thy grace, so that we may frequently and gratefully accept Thy invitation to partake of Thy Holy Supper and become rejoicing partakers of Thy heavenly bounty -- forgiveness of sins, light in darkness, comfort in sorrow, strength in weakness, help in distress, rest in labor, certainty in doubt, and protection in danger. Yes, Lord Jesus, let us taste in Thy Supper Thy heavenly goodness. Amen.

XVI. COMMUNION COUNSEL TO THE SICK

The benefits which Christ wishes to confer upon the believing communicant must make it most desirable for the sick to partake of it, particularly for those who are about to depart this life for eternity. Holy Communion in its very nature is a powerful means of strengthening the dying Christian's faith and assuring him of a blessed departure from this life. Since the believer is so intimately united with his Redeemer by partaking of His body and blood this already is a pledge that Jesus will fulfill in him the promise, "Where I am, there shall also My servant be." But it is also quite apparent that the believer upon his sick-bed should use due diligence so to prepare himself that he may derive the benefits God has intended for him.

We should realize that the mere partaking of Holy Communion, without faith, will bring no benefit. It is necessary to emphasize this self-evident truth in this connection because so many hold the wrong opinion that, if a person but receives the Lord's Supper before his death, salvation is assured him; and this false idea then prevents the proper preparation of many sick for Communion by sincere repentance for sin and a heartfelt longing for forgiveness. Alas, how great is the number of those who in this false hope of salvation depart this life to step before the just judge, who cannot but reject them from His eternal kingdom because they died in impenitence and unbelief despite the fact that they partook of Christ's body and blood before their death!

The Christian whom God has visited with illness should also well bear in mind that he must not postpone receiving the

Sacrament till the weakening powers of his mind prevent due preparation. Before your mental strength has diminished, you should turn your special attention to your past life and conscientiously review it in the light of God's Law and of our Savior's atoning death; and may such a searching examination with the help of the Holy Spirit lead you to sincere repentance and the honest desire to right whatever wrong you have done, as much as lies in your power. But may such heart-searching also lead you to Him who died that you may live forever and impel you to take hold of Him as the safe anchor of hope amidst the tempestuous seas of fear and doubt and accusations that threaten to engulf you when once your conscience is fully awakened to realize the nature and consequences of your disobedience. Cling to the Lord Jesus by trusting in His Word and promises; do not permit Satan to lead you to believe that Jesus is not willing to save you. Have no fear that He will ever change His mind who said when He was still here upon earth in visible form, "Him that cometh to Me I will in no wise cast out." Relying upon His invitation and assurance say:

> Rock of Ages, cleft for me,
> Let me hide myself in Thee.
> Let the water and the blood
> From Thy riven side which flowed
> Be of sin the double cure,
> Cleanse me from its guilt and power.

And when the Holy Spirit has brought you to such a penitent and believing state of heart, permit nothing to hold you back from the Lord's Table; for you will be a most welcome guest, and great will be the blessings you will receive. By God's grace you will experience, as you never did before, the sweet conviction that all your sins are forgiven and forgotten, that Jesus is your Savior, Guide, and Protector, that nothing can separate you from God's love in Christ Jesus, and that even before your departure from this life there is prepared for you a mansion in your heavenly Father's home.

PRAYER

Heavenly Father, it hath pleased Thee to cast me on this sickbed. I know that Thou hast only a kind and loving purpose in view in depriving me of my health, and willingly I bow to Thy will and submit myself in patience to Thy guidance.

I know that I have often sinned against Thy will and deserved Thy chastisement; but I come to Thee with a contrite and penitent heart and ask Thee graciously to forgive me for the sake of Jesus' merits. And that I may be the more certain of Thy pardon, I desire to partake of my Savior's body and blood in the Sacrament. Gracious Father, I firmly believe that Thy dear Son gave His body and shed His blood for the remission of my sins, and by eating His body and drinking His blood I desire to become more certain that all His merits are actually imputed to me, just as if I myself had suffered and died and atoned for my sins. Dearest Father, I believe this, but my own flesh and Satan seek to undermine my faith by instilling doubt into my heart, and for this reason I pray Thee, lay Thy special blessing upon my Communion that my weak faith may be strengthened as I receive this pledge and token of Thine abiding love and mercy which Thou so graciously hast granted me in the Holy Supper.

O grant that my Communion may redound to my lasting blessing. Give me patience in suffering, courage under trials, comfort in sorrow, faith in temptation, certainty in doubt, and hope in despondency. Enable me in the strength of this heavenly food and drink to overcome all my enemies and in the light of its blessed assurances never to lose sight of my eternal goal.

Heavenly Father, I commit my body and soul with childlike confidence into Thy gracious hands since through Jesus' blood and redemption they have become Thine own, and I trustingly await the blessed hour when Thou wilt redeem me from these earthly toils and guide me into full and perfect liberty with all Christ's own in Thy heaven of spotless purity and unalloyed bliss. O Father in heaven, keep me in this faith for Jesus' sake. Amen.

XVII. ADDITIONAL COMMUNION PRAYERS

I.

Oh, the height, the depth, the length and the breadth of Thy love, O God! Angels cannot reach, much less can human understanding fathom it. Only permit me Lord, to look at it and wonder, to admire and adore that which I readily realize as being incomprehensible. Thy love is a subject with the pondering of which I do not know where to begin; and once begun, I do not know where to end. Thy love for us began long before we existed, long before the foundation of the world. Yes, Lord, Thou didst love us when there was no eye to pity, even when we were less than nothing. Was there ever an eye enamored of deformity? Yet, when sin had so defiled us that from the crown of our head to the sole of our feet there was no soundness in us, Thou didst lovingly cast Thy mantle over us to hide our shame. When we lay in our blood, expecting nothing but death, Thou saidst unto us, "Live," and didst pour wine and oil into our wounds; Thou didst clothe us with white raiment, deck us with jewels, graciously espouse us unto Thyself, and receive us into Thy bosom. So great was Thy love for us that our extreme unworthiness could not abate it, but only increase and inflame it.

Herein hast Thou commended Thy love to us that, while we were yet sinners, Christ died for us. Thou didst pity us when we hated Thee; and even when our hand was uplifted against Thee, Thy arms were opened to receive and embrace us. Surely never was love like unto Thine, not only passing knowledge, but wonder and admiration.

O Lord Jesus, how am I lost in amazement when I see how Thy love has drawn Thee towards us poor sinners! How unspeakable that love which could bring Thee down from the glory of the highest heavens and the bosom of Thy eternal Father to this world, to this home of sorrow and death! How amazing Thy love which could cause Thee to spend Thy life, from the manger to the cross, in sorrow and grief that we might be happy! Thy love is stronger than death and deeper than hell, higher than heaven and longer than the earth. But not content with this manifestation of Thy love, Thou dost further in Thy Supper give us a cup of blessings, full of blessings, good measure, pressed down, and running over; nor is there fear of exhausting it. If we want pardon, here it is. If we want peace, it is there. If we want humility, patience, light, strength, comfort -- all these gifts which Christ hath purchased with His blood He freely bestows upon us in the Holy Supper as He gives us His body and blood. What is the manna that fed Israel in the wilderness, what the water that gushed forth from the rock to quench their thirst, to this food and drink here offered our souls? What is the pool of Bethesda, what are the waters of Siloam to this blessed fountain, which cleanseth from all sin and heals all spiritual diseases?

O Lord, what can I render unto Thee for all these gifts of Thy love? My love is so cold, and my services are so inadequate. I must blush that I am so sparing in my appreciation.

O Lord Jesus, take me just as I am and make me wholly Thine; grant me faith to expect, and patience to wait for, that hour when I shall stand before Thy throne and serve Thee day and night in Thy temple and when Thou shalt take full possession of my heart and attune my lips to sing Thine unending praise. Amen.

II.

"My Lord and my God" Only enable me to say that, and I ask no more, Lord Jesus. Others may think themselves happy that they can say, "My houses, my lands, my possessions, my treasures"; but, blessed Jesus, I shall deem myself unutterably rich and unspeakably happy if I may but lay hold on Thee as my Lord and my God. It is this proprietorship wherein my life and happiness consist. Life would be worth nothing to me if I could not say, "My Lord!" There would be no comfort for me if Thou wert not my God.

And now Thou comest to me in Thy holy Sacrament and givest me a sure pledge that Thou art mine. To support my tottering faith, Thou assurest me that Thou art my Savior, and to remove all doubt, Thou givest me a token more sure than if Thou wouldst permit me actually to put my finger into the prints of the nails and to thrust my hand into Thy side. And all this Thou dost to prove that Thou art not only the Author, but also the Finisher of my faith, that Thou dost not despise small things, that Thou wilt not break the bruised reed nor quench the smoking flax, that Thou wilt pity the weakness of my faith, forgive my unbelieving and distrustful attitude, banish my guilty fears, confirm my wavering hopes, and enable me to say with well-grounded confidence, "My Lord and my God." Hear me for Thy mercy's sake. Amen.

III.

Lord Jesus, no one but my God could know, no one but my

Savior could forgive, my obstinate unbelief and come to my help as Thou dost in the holy Sacrament. I am astonished at my unbelief and at Thy patience and long-suffering. I scarcely know which to wonder at most, the weakness of my faith or the strength of Thy love. How surprising that Thou shouldst stoop so low as to give me Thy body and blood in Holy Communion to satisfy the needs of my wayward heart!

O Lord Jesus, I will have no God but Thee. No other Lord shall henceforth have dominion over me; and I humbly hope that no circumstance, however dark and discouraging, will ever again tempt me to question the power, the grace, or the faithfulness of my Lord and my God. As the hart panteth after the water-brooks, so grant that my soul may eagerly long for Thee. Amen.

IV.

Dear Savior, I now again present myself at Thy table. Here I have before seen Thee in Thy beauty; here Thou hast opened for me the treasures of Thy grace and with rich variety satisfied me with good things. Here Thou hast, with no more apparent provision than a few loaves, fed many thousands that otherwise must have perished in the wilderness. Here many a spiritual cripple has found his true Bethesda; here, too, in the breaking of bread, Thou hast revealed Thyself to Thy sorrowing disciples to their inexpressible joy.

Hither therefore I come in the humble hope of having closer fellowship with Thee, Lord Jesus. O Thou who canst have compassion on the ignorant and them that have gone astray, cast me not away from Thy presence. Send me not empty away. Disperse the cloud that has separated me from Thee and manifest Thyself to me so sweetly that I shall be forced to cry in faith and grateful admiration, "My Lord and my God." Amen.

V.

Blessed Jesus, Thou Bread of Life, how many titles hast Thou given Thyself to express Thy love and tenderness to us and to bring home to us the necessities of us poor and perishing sinners! When we were full of wounds and putrefying sores, what we most wanted was a physician, compassionate and skilful; one that could be touched by a feeling of our infirmities and was mighty to save. And it was sweet music to our souls to hear Thee say: "The Spirit of the Lord is upon Me because He hath ... sent Me to heal the broken-hearted." When we were dead in sins and condemned to temporal death and eternal damnation, Thou camest to us with the blessed assurance: "I am the Resurrection and the Life; he that believeth in Me, though he were dead, yet shall he live; and whosoever liveth and believeth in Me shall never die." When we were distressed because of our sins and sought to flee from the presence of a righteous and avenging God, Thou didst assure us that Thou art our Mediator, ready to turn away the flames of God's wrath. When we were groping about like blind men seeking God and finding Him not, Thou didst come to bring us the welcome tidings: "I am the Way, the Truth, and the Life; no man cometh unto the Father but by Me." When we wandered about like lost sheep in the wilderness of this world's dangers and wants, without food and drink, Thou didst rejoice our fainting hearts by saying, "I am the Good Shepherd." These and many other titles dost

Thou give Thyself to tell us that all we need we can find in Thee and that Thou art accessible to the poorest and most lowly among us. Grant me to find ever greater riches in Thee and to this end bless my contemplated Communion. Amen.

VI.

Blessed Jesus, why dost Thou show much greater love to us than to the angels? Thou showest us favors which angels never knew. We are feasted by Thy love, our hungry souls Thou feedest with good things. Prodigal-like we had left home, wasted our substance, and reduced ourselves to beggary and want; but here at Thy table Thou receivest us as Thine own and biddest us eat the children's bread. Thou givest us Thyself as food for our souls and yieldest us the most substantial refreshment. Pardon for sins, the favor of God, peace of conscience, a clean heart, a right spirit, grace to help, and the hope of glory, these are only some of the blessings Thou bringest to us as we partake of Thy body and Thy blood in Thy Supper. Yes, all we need Thou givest us at Thy table, and thus Thou makest us, who are poorer than Lazarus, rich and us, who are full of sores, well and whole.

And now, Lord Jesus, that Thou hast brought me into Thy banqueting hall and set me at Thy rich table, I see all things are ready but myself. My heart is indifferent when it should rejoice. I am grieved and ashamed that my appetite is no keener in view of Thy provisions; that Thou shouldst set before me bread so nourishing, so strengthening, so enlivening and that I should be so listless, as if I did not care whether I partook of it or not. I have long groaned under this melancholy ailment; I have often deplored that my heart should be so sluggish and cold; I have labored to stir up more fervent desires; and now again I come to Thee and beseech Thee to enable me to open my mouth wide and to enlarge the desires of my soul, to stir my stupid breast to long after Thee and graciously to fill me with good things; then, O dearest Savior, shall a soul that was ready to perish bless Thy holy name. Amen.

VII.

Dear Savior, with Thine own lips Thou hast told us: "The Father Himself loveth you." The feast of Thy Supper is proof sufficient of this love; for if He had not loved me, would He have done such great things for me through Thee? Would He have sent Thee into the world to save me? Would He have bruised Thee and put Thee to grief and made Thy soul an offering for my sin? If He had not loved me, would He have called me and inclined and enabled me to heed the call to come? If He had not loved me, would He have brought me into His banqueting hall? I was perishing with hunger, and all through my own fault; I had left His house and squandered His bounties; and if He had left me to starve, He would have done right, for I had done wickedly; but instead He rescued me from death, and now He bids me eat heavenly food such as is not given to angels. Yes, the evidences of His love are clear, but I so long to see more the effects of His love and its influence upon my heart. I would have my heart be more humbled and broken for sin; I wish to trust in God more implicitly; I wish to have my love more vigorous and fervent. I long to have Him who toucheth the mountains and they smoke to touch my frozen heart with a live coal from His altar that, while I meditate upon His amazing love to me, I may feel my love to Him kindled into a bright and living flame. I would not only profess my love and gratitude to Him, but I desire strength to love Him in deed and in truth.

To this end I am coming to my Savior's table, which His and the Father's love has spread that the Father's and my Savior's love may be indelibly impressed upon my heart, so that I may have strength to ward off all temptations of devil, world, and flesh. For I know that from the Lord's altar I shall have to go out again into the world, where this and that thing will entice me and where I shall meet with many things that will solicit my affections. When such solicitations and temptations beset me, let me hear Thee whispering to my heart as Thou remindest me of Thy Passion and its memorial, "Lovest thou Me more than these?" and thus keep me from falling.

O Lord Jesus, grant that my Communion may be the means to direct my heart into Thy love and that of the Father more and more. O Thou who hast loved me and hast hitherto given me consolation and good hope through grace comfort my heart and establish it in every good word and work for Thy mercy's sake. Amen.

VIII.

Blessed Savior, in the night in which Thou didst eat the last Passover with Thy disciples, Thou saidst to them: "With desire have I desired to eat this Passover with you." Such a desire to partake of the Holy Supper should fill my heart whenever the table is spread. But have I this desire in the measure that it should be found in me? Dearest Savior, Thou knowest better than I can tell Thee that I must blush for shame because my desire is not greater than it is. Only too often other things interpose themselves between Thee and me. For one thing, there is sin. O Lord, take away mine iniquity and receive me graciously. Take all sin away, dear Lord, spare not a right hand nor a right eye. Out with it! Off with it! There is no sin so dear to my sinful flesh but I will sacrifice it by Thy grace in order to come nearer to Thee. And there is the world. O teach me to see that the love of the world cannot live in the same heart with the love of my Savior. And then there is doubt and unbelief, which so often spoil my appetite for Thy Supper. I long after Thee, and yet there is a strange unwillingness within me or shyness and diffidence to draw near to Thy table. I find my heart so dead, my thoughts so wandering, my love so cold, and there are so many things in which I have sadly failed that I feel unworthy and fear that I may eat and drink judgment to myself. O dearest Jesus, make me ashamed of such unbelieving fears; do not let me insult Thy love and goodness by doubting Thy precious promises and by acting as if I thought Thee untrustworthy and Thy Word not fit to be depended upon. Teach me to put my whole trust in Thy promises. Help me to say: "I am a poor helpless creature; whither shall I go but to Thee, the Rock of Ages? I am a poor guilty creature; whither shall I flee but to the Lamb of God, who taketh away the sin of the world? I am a poor tempted creature; where shall I seek refuge but with my merciful and faithful High Priest, who, having been tempted in all things like as we are, can be touched by the feeling of mine infirmities?" Lord, I flee to Thee; graciously receive me. Amen.

IX.

O Jesus, Thou hast done all things that it was possible to do to convince me of Thy faithfulness. It was no worthiness in me that led Thee to make me the object of Thy love at first; and why should I think that Thy love is not as free now as it was then? Lord Jesus, Thou hast good reason to upbraid me for my doubts and indifference; for Thou hast ever been ready to bear my griefs and carry my sorrows. Oh, grant me grace humbly to throw myself at Thy feet and help me by Thy mercy that my Communion may bring me ever nearer to Thee and that I may long ever more intensely for Thy presence. Grant that, as I depart from Thy table, my heart may be enlarged and full in surrender to Thee, help that I may pray more earnestly for holiness, and make me strong successfully to overcome every temptation that may beset my path with the strength that Thou art ready to give me at Thy table. Amen.

X.

Lord, I come to Thy table not because I am worthy, but because Thou art rich in grace and dost promise that the needy shall not be forgotten and that the expectations of the poor shall not perish. I know that Thou wilt do as Thou hast said: Thou wilt pity a poor, needy, perishing creature and fill it out of the ocean of Thy mercy. As I come to the feast of Thy appointment, Thou wilt not fail to display to me Thy fullness and liberality. Thou wilt surely open the doors of Thy treasury and allow me access to Thine unsearchable riches. Thy Word doth assure me that in all ages Thou hast bestowed these riches upon the poor and needy without money and without price. Let me not go away from Thy table without alms, without a crumb of Thy children's bread, seeing there is bread enough and to spare. Oh, let me not return from Thy fountain of blessing unrefreshed! Thou hast promised to pour water upon the thirsty and floods upon the dry ground; and see, Lord, there is no one more dry, more poor, more needy than I am. Lord, make me as thirsty as I am dry, as humble as I am poor, and as sensible as I am needy. Deal not with me according to my sense of need, which is small, but deal with me according to my actual wants and Thy royal bounty, which is unlimited. Hear my humble prayer, dear Jesus. Amen.

XI.

My Lord and Savior, oh, that I would feel my poverty and want as I should feel it: that I am drowned in debt to the Law and justice of God and have not one cent to pay it; that I am destitute of every thing that is good and can do nothing to please God and am unworthy of the least of His mercies! Oh, that I could only be content to trust wholly to Thy righteousness to justify me and for Thy Spirit and grace to renew and sanctify my nature! Help me in my weakness, dear Savior. Amen.

XII.

Lord, I am poor, but in Thee are treasured up unsearchable riches and inexhaustible fullness to satisfy all my needs; I am naked, but Thou, Lord Jesus, hast a robe of righteousness that is sufficient to cover me and a whole world of sinners; I am a starving creature, but Thou art the Bread of Life and the

Water of Life for my soul; I am foolish and ignorant, but Thou hast infinite wisdom to teach and guide me; I am laden with guilt, but Thy sacrifice is sufficient to atone for it; I have strong lusts and desires, but Thou hast a royal power to subdue them; I am in much darkness, but Thou art the Light of the world; I am under fears and discouragements, but Thou art the Consolation of Israel; I am wounded and sick, but Thou hast balm to heal me; I am under a burden of debt, but Thou art my Surety, rich and fully able to pay; I am in prison, but Thou openest the prison doors and loosest my bonds; I am fatherless, but Thou art mine everlasting Father; Law, Satan, and my own conscience accuse me, but Thou art my Advocate before the throne of divine justice. Therefore I flee to Thee, Lord Jesus, for refuge and put my whole confidence in Thee. Amen.

XIII.

O my Savior, what great encouragement it brings my needy soul that as a surety and pledge of Thy goodness and merits Thou hast instituted the holy Sacrament, to which Thou most graciously invitest me as a guest, thus preparing a table before me in the presence of all mine enemies as an assurance that Thou wilt never leave me nor forsake me. Grant me grace to find at Thy table all the strength and comfort Thou hast intended for me, for Thy mercy's sake. Amen.

Printed in the United States
48088LVS00004B/31-105